Where Are Your Toes?

Written by Barry Hoag
Illustrated by Cailyn Hoag

Xulon Press

Copyright © 2015 by Barry Hoag illustrated by Cailyn Hoag

WHERE ARE YOUR TOES?
by Barry Hoag illustrated by Cailyn Hoag

Printed in the United States of America

ISBN 9781498433419

All rights reserved solely by the author. The author guarantees all contents are original and do not infringe upon the legal rights of any other person or work. No part of this book may be reproduced in any form without the permission of the author. The views expressed in this book are not necessarily those of the publisher.

Unless otherwise indicated, Scripture quotations are taken from the New Revised Standard Version (NRSV). Copyright © 1989 the Division of Christian Education of the National Council of the Churches of Christ in the United States of America.

www.xulonpress.com

Thank you to my wife who is my rock and support for my ministry. Without her there would be no ministry. Also, thank you to my sister-in-law, Rev. Dr. Belle Drake who has taught me much about God and ministry.

WHERE ARE YOUR TOES?

Then God said, "Let us make humankind in our image, according to our likeness... Genesis 1:26

When we walk, our toes are out in front of us. Where ever we go our toes get there first.

...but if we walk in the light as he himself is in the light, we have fellowship with one another... I John 1:7

We should know ahead of time where we want our toes to go.

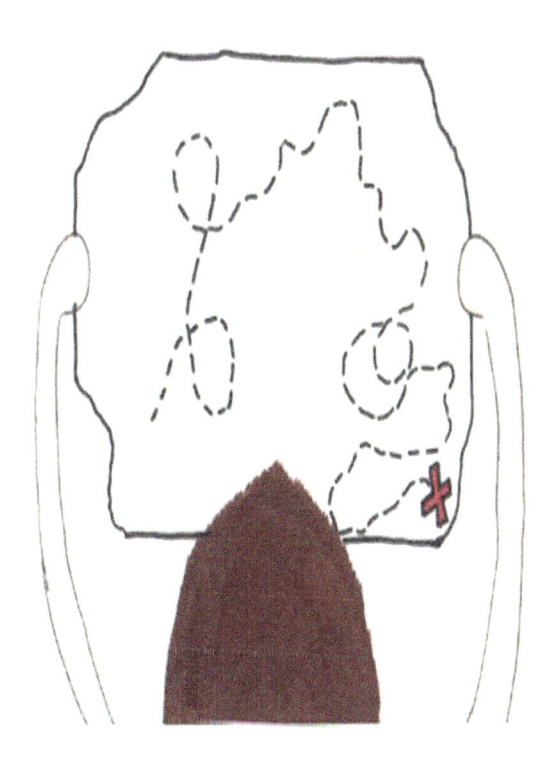

Your word is a lamp unto my feet and a light to my path. PSALM 119:105

If we love and believe in Jesus our toes will lead us down the path toward Heaven!

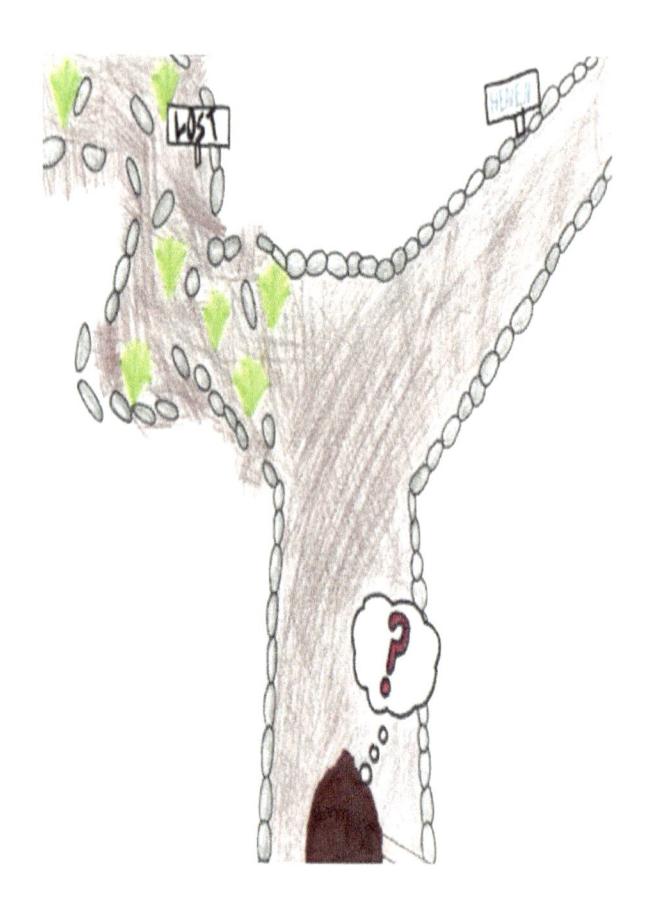

For surely I know the plans I have for you, says the Lord, plans for your welfare and not for harm, to give you a future with hope. Jeremiah 29:11

Our toes go everywhere we go. Let me show you.

...for we walk by faith and not by sight. 2 Corinthians 5:7

When we ride our bike our toes go real fast.

Then go quickly and tell his disciples, He has been raised from the dead… Matthew 28:7

When we jump up and down our toes go up and down.

Let them praise his name with dancing, making melody to him with tambourine and lyre! Psalm 149:3

When we are happy our toes wiggle with excitement.

... "How beautiful are the feet of those who bring good news."
Romans 10:15

When we are sad our toes go real slow.

Blessed are those who mourn, for they will be comforted.
Matthew 5:4

Sometimes we wander off the right path and we stub our toes.

Though we stumble, we shall not fall headlong, for the LORD holds us by the hand. Psalm 37:24

Sometimes we make bad choices that take us off the path to Heaven and we get toe-lio.

Make me to know your ways, O LORD; teach me your paths. Psalm 25:4

When we deliberately take our toes away from Heaven's path, we can get toe-mane poisoning.

All we like sheep have gone astray; we have all turned away...
Isaiah 53:6

Toe-mane poisoning can happen when we are angry or we are mean to others.

Put away from you all bitterness and wrath and anger and wrangling and slander, together with all malice, and be kind to one another, tenderhearted, forgiving one another, as God in Christ has forgiven you. Ephesians 4:31-32

So how do we get our toes back on the right path toward Heaven?

Trust in the LORD with all your heart, and do not rely on your own insight. In all your ways acknowledge him, and he will make straight your paths. Proverbs 3:5-6

Before we go to bed at night we can look down at our toes. Say: "Toes where have you been all day?"

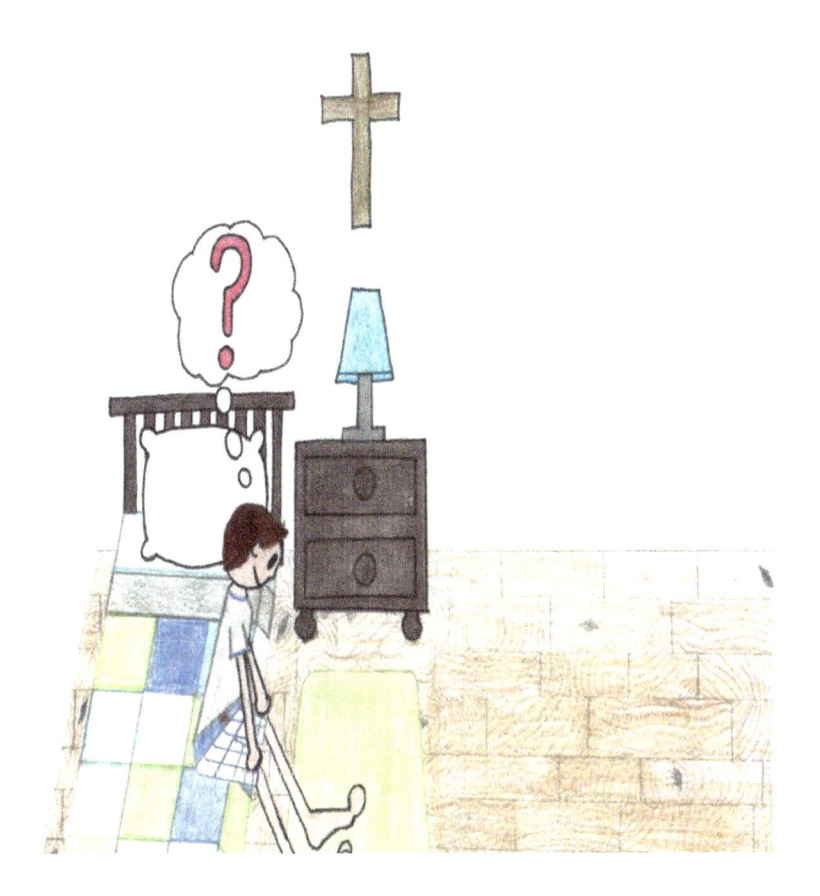

My dear children, I write these things to you so that you may not sin. But if anybody does sin, we have an advocate with the Father, Jesus Christ, the righteous; 1 John 2:1

Remember all the places you have been that day. Ask your toes if they were on the path to Heaven all day.

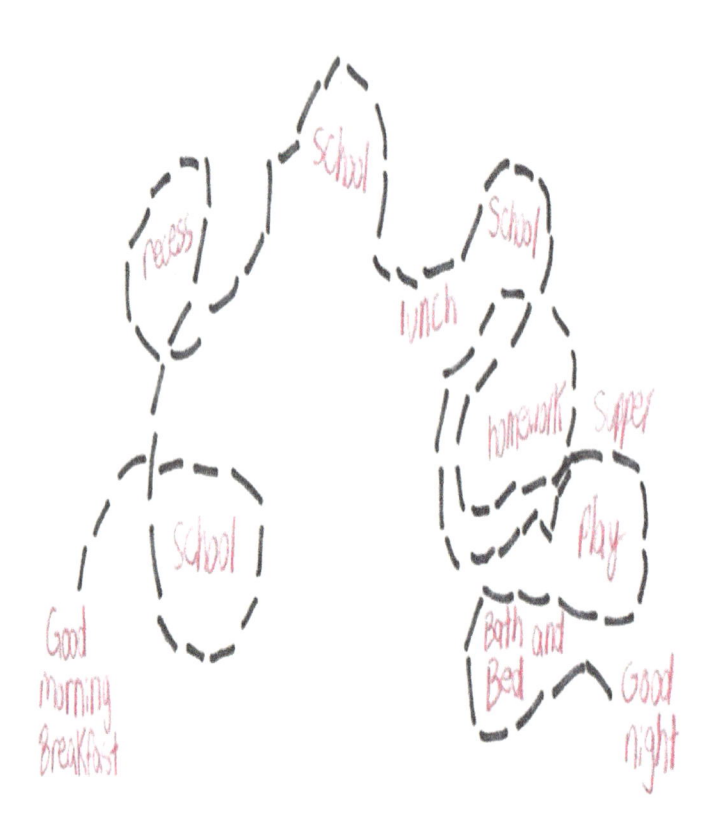

Examine yourselves to see whether you are living in the faith. Test yourselves. Do you not realize that Jesus Christ is in you? Unless, indeed, you fail to meet the test! 2 Corinthians 13:5

If our toes were on a different path, how do they get back on the right path to Heaven?

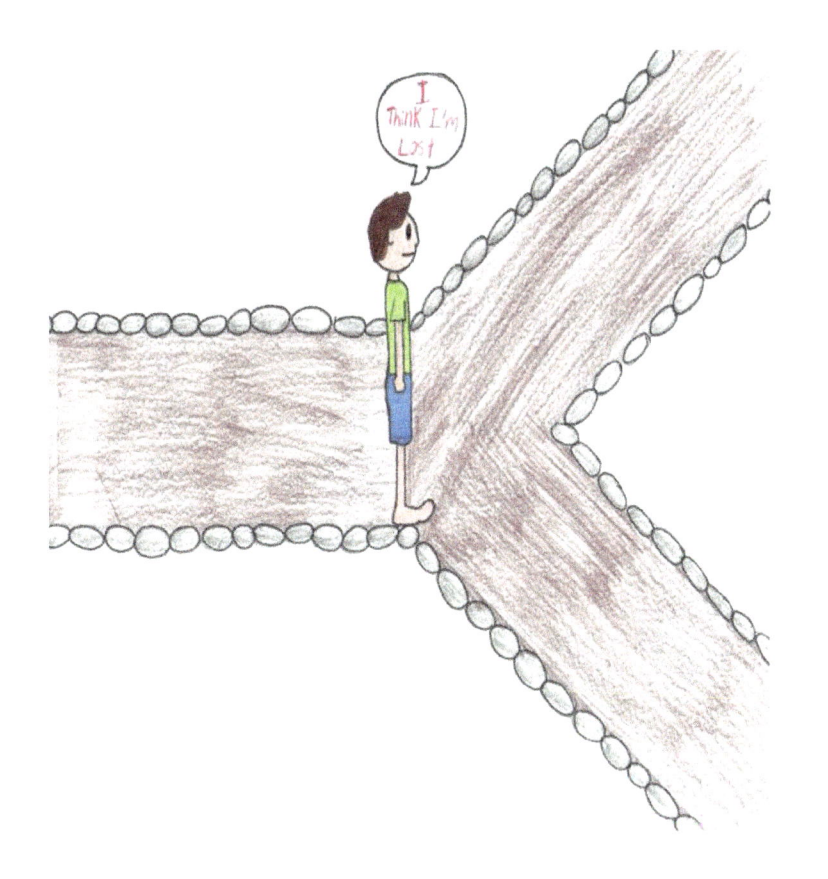

You show me the path of life… Psalm 16:11

When we say our night time prayers, we can ask God to help our toes find the right path.

If we confess our sins, He who is faithful and just will forgive us our sins…1 John 1:9

Because God loves us and forgives us, He will guide our toes to the right path.

For by grace you have been saved through faith, and this is not your own doing; it is the gift of God. Ephesians 2:8

No one or nothing can ever keep us from the love of God or the right path to Heaven.

This is not the end but the beginning!

...nor anything else in all creation, will be able to separate us from the love of God in Christ Jesus our Lord. Romans 8:39

My prayer for you is that this book may help guide you to the path to Heaven. God loves you and He wants to be in your life.
Pooh PaPa

You shall love the Lord your God with all your heart, and with all your soul, and with all your mind, and with all your strength. Mark 12:30

CPSIA information can be obtained at www.ICGtesting.com
Printed in the USA
LVOW02*0012280515

440151LV00001B/1/P